YOUR KNOWLEDGE HAS VALUE

- We will publish your bachelor's and
  master's thesis, essays and papers

- Your own eBook and book -
  sold worldwide in all relevant shops

- Earn money with each sale

**Upload your text at www.GRIN.com
and publish for free**

Galina Bernhardt

Noise Patterns in industrial Micro Computed Tomography

GRIN Publishing

Bibliographic information published by the German National Library:

The German National Library lists this publication in the National Bibliography; detailed bibliographic data are available on the Internet at http://dnb.dnb.de .

This book is copyright material and must not be copied, reproduced, transferred, distributed, leased, licensed or publicly performed or used in any way except as specifically permitted in writing by the publishers, as allowed under the terms and conditions under which it was purchased or as strictly permitted by applicable copyright law. Any unauthorized distribution or use of this text may be a direct infringement of the author s and publisher s rights and those responsible may be liable in law accordingly.

Imprint:

Copyright © 2010 GRIN Verlag GmbH
Print and binding: Books on Demand GmbH, Norderstedt Germany
ISBN: 978-3-640-83856-1

This book at GRIN:

http://www.grin.com/en/e-book/165584/noise-patterns-in-industrial-micro-computed-tomography

GRIN - Your knowledge has value

Since its foundation in 1998, GRIN has specialized in publishing academic texts by students, college teachers and other academics as e-book and printed book. The website www.grin.com is an ideal platform for presenting term papers, final papers, scientific essays, dissertations and specialist books.

Visit us on the internet:

http://www.grin.com/

http://www.facebook.com/grincom

http://www.twitter.com/grin_com

Fachhochschule
Nordwestschweiz

Noise Patterns in industrial Computed Tomography

STAGE II

Galina Bernhardt

Student
Mechatronik Trinational

Abstract

Computer Tomography (CT) systems are used to produced images that are finding increasing use in medicine and mineralogy as in the Natural History Museum. In order to maximise the system performance, the images or scans, must have high quality. Ideally, the physical CT system should preserve the image quality. However, in reality, various physical processes degrade the quality of these images, producing noise and artefacts.

The goal of this work is to understand the noise and artefacts in high-resolution imaging application of micro computer tomography (micro-CT). The project specifically looked at determining:

I.   How micro-CT scan parameters be optimised to reduce noise, and

II.   Which of the many commonly used noise reduction algorithms produce the best results, and

III.   How current and exposure effect each other.

Experiments were carried out to obtain the raw data – images / scans for the study. Theoretical models were then implemented on the raw data to analyse and better understand the noise and artefacts in the images.

This work provides a better understanding of both the fundamental performance (i.e. image quality) of the micro-CT system, and the assessment of user-defined parameters that could be used to optimise the performance of the micro-CT systems.

These contributions will not only save time, money and resources, which will ultimately lead to better image quality (greater accuracy)

Section 1 introduces the background and then the recent developments of the Natural History Museum, London. This is then followed by a brief description of Computer Tomography (CT), covering basic concepts of this technology with emphasis on industrial CT and Micro-CT. Noise and artefacts, covering the difference between noise and artefacts, and the problems faced – during this project - in the operation of computer tomography are explained in detail. Additionally, fundamental principles of low and high pass filters for digital signal processing are covered

The results and summary are discussed in detail in sections 2 and 3.

Die von Computer-Tomographie (CT)-Systemen erzeugten Bilder finden immer mehr Anwendung: Ob in der Medizin oder der Mineralogie, wie im Natural History Museum. Um die System-Leistung voll ausschöpfen zu können, müssen die Aufnahmen oder Scans von höchster Qualität sein. Im Idealfall darf die eigentliche Apparatur des CT-Systems die Bildqualität nicht beeinträchtigen. Dies ist allerdings im Alltag noch immer die Schwachstelle: Die physikalischen Prozesse beeinflussen die Qualität der Aufnahmen, indem sie Rauschen und Artefakte erzeugen.

Ziel dieser Arbeit ist es, das Rauschen und Artefakte bei hochauflösenden Bild-Anwendungen in der Mikro- Computertomographie (Mikro-CT) nachvollziehen zu können. Das Projekt möchte vor allem untersuchen:

I.   Wie die Aufnahme-Parameter der Mikro-CT optimiert werden können, um Rauschen zu reduzieren und

II.   Welche der üblicherweise verwendeten Algorithmen zur Reduzierung des Rauschens die besten Ergebnisse zeigen, und

III.   Wie der Spannung und Belichtungszeit sich gegenseitig beeinflussen.

Es wurden zahlreiche Experimente durchgeführt, um die Rohdaten, die Aufnahmen / Scans, für diese Studie zu erhalten. Danach wurden theoretische Modelle an diesen Rohdaten angewandt, um das Rauschen und Artefakte der Aufnahmen besser verstehen zu können.

Diese Arbeit liefert ein besseres Verständnis für beides: für die grundsätzlichen Leistungen (z.B. Aufnahme-Qualität) des Mikro-CT-Systems und die Bewertung der benutzerdefinierten Parameter, die verwendet werden können, um die Leistung der Mikro-CT-Systeme zu verbessern.

Diese Fokussierung wird nicht nur Zeit, Geld und Ressourcen einsparen, ihr Ziel ist vielmehr eine bessere Bildqualität (höhere Genauigkeit).

Abschnitt 1 führt in die Hintergründe der Problematik ein und berichtet anschließend über den neuesten Stand der Entwicklung im Natural History Museum in London. Dem folgt eine kurze Beschreibung der Computertomographie (CT), in der die grundlegenden Konzepte dieser Technologie angesprochen werden, wobei das Hauptaugenmerk auf der industriellen und der Mikro-CT liegen soll. Weiter geht es mit Rauschen und Artefakten und der Frage, was eigentlich der Unterschied zwischen beidem ist. Außerdem werden natürlich die während dieses Projektes aufgetretenen Probleme in der Anwendung der Computertomographie detailliert erklärt. Darüber hinaus wird auf Tief- und Hochpassfilter in der digitalen Signalverarbeitung Bezug genommen.

Die Ergebnisse und die Zusammenfassung werden detailliert im Abschnitt 2 und 3 besprochen.

Table of contents

Table of Figures

Table of Tables

1   Introduction

The first section introduces the background and then the recent developments of the Natural History Museum, London. This is then followed by a brief description of Computer Tomography (CT), covering basic concepts of this technology with emphasis on industrial CT and Micro-CT.

The difference between noise and artefacts are discussed in detail and the problems faced – during this project - in the operation of computer tomography are explained. Additionally, fundamental principles of low and high pass filters for digital signal processing are covered.

1.1   The Natural History Museum London (NHM)

The Natural History Museum (NHM) is located in South Kensington, London and is one of the biggest Natural History Museums in the world. The museum both exhibits (for the general public) and actively researches on:

- animals
- plants
- ecosystems
- geology
- palaeontology
- climatology(Wikipedia Natural History Museum)

1.1.1   The beginning of the British Museum (NHM London)

The NHM started with a young English boy named Hans Sloane who was interested in Botany. Sloane during his education in medicine spent some of his time in Europe. On his way to Paris he met the chemist Nicolas Lemery; in the French capital he visited the Jardin du Roi and frequented the Charite´ hospital. He also heard lectures on botany and anatomy. After completion of his degree, Sloan soon became famous as a physician as well as a botanist.

Figure 1: Portrait of Hans Sloane

When Christopher Monck, second duke of Albemarle, was appointed governor of Jamaica, he appointed Sloane to accompany him to the island as his personal physician. The expedition was of great value to Sloane, not only giving him first-hand experience of a relatively little-known island but also enabling him to search for new drugs. The description of the voyage and the observations on the inhabitants, diseases, plants, animals, some of which he brought back alive, and meteorology of the West Indies make Sloane's book on Jamaica valuable even today. The duchess of Albemarle was suffering from the first stages of the mental illness which turned to madness later. As a result the duke became an alcoholic and died within a year of arriving in Jamaica. Sloane escorted the duchess back to England in 1689. He brought with him collections of plants, animals, fossils, minerals and earth and a large quantity of note and drawings (Thackray and Press).

His house, now 3 Bloomsbury Place W.C.I, where he lived from 1695 until 1742, soon became so full that he was obliged to rent the adjoining house, No. 4, as well. In 1712 he bought the manor house at Chelsea, although he did not retire to live there until 1742 when all his collections followed him.

From the early days of the century Sloane's museum had been an object of interest not only to British scholars and men of science but also to foreigners, many of whom were urged not to leave the country without seeing it. Sloane's doors were always opened to the visitors. He always wanted the public to benefit from his collection(Thackray and Press).

Sloane died on 11 January 1753. In his will he offered all these treasures to the British nation, on condition that £20 000 was paid to his daughters, who might have expected to inherit the valuable collection. After Sloane's death on January 11, 1753 the trustees whom he had appointed met; the matter was brought before parliament, which received Royal Assent for the Act which enabled Sloane's collection to be acquired and a suitable building purchased to house it. King George II was one of the interested parties mentioned in Sloane's will. The King decided to buy some other collections as well. On the 7th June 1753 King George II established the Sloane, Cotton and Harleian collections as the British Museum for general use and benefit of the public.

Figure 2: Montagu House, Bloomsbury (Hubpages London)

On Monday the 15th of January 1759 the door of the British Museum were opened for the public. Many donations were made during the years and the British Museum in Bloomsbury become crowded with specimens. A decision to separate the Natural History collection from the rest was made. In 1880 new building in South Kensington was completed, where the departments of Mineralogy, Botany and Geology were move (Thackray and Press).

On the 18th of April 1881, the museum was officially named "British Museum "(Natural history)". In 1992 the name was changed to The Natural History Museum because of the confusion as many visitors used to come expecting to see Egyptian mummies and other artefacts of ancient civilization (Thackray and Press).

The NHM has always been at the forefront of newest technologies and their applications such as for analyzing specimens. For example, the first electron microscope was constructed in the 1939s and the Museum purchased its first model, a transmission electron microscope, in 1965 (Thackray and Press).

1.1.2   NHM in the 21st Century

The Museum is an exempt charity and a non-departmental public body sponsored by the Department of Culture, Media and Sport.

The museum contains more than 70 million specimens and has a library with very rare books – with great historical and scientific value. The museum's staff stands at 843, of whom approximately 315 are scientists that devote the majority of their time to the collections and research.

Figure 3: The Natural History Museum, London (Wikipedia Natural History Museum)

The Museum is also a world-renowned centre of research, specialising in taxonomy, identification and conservation of specimens (Wikipedia Natural History Museum).

1.2   Computed Tomography(CT) – Introduction

Academia and users refer to computer tomography by many names:

*   Computerized axial transverse scanning

*   Computerized axial tomography (CAT)

*   X-ray computed tomography (X-ray CT)

*   Computed/computerized tomography (CT) (Karthikeyan and Deepa)

For discussions in this work, computed tomography (CT) will be used.

Computed Tomography is a widely used imaging technique, with special emphasis on medical applications. Tomography uses the radiographic images of the object obtained from different angles. Using an algorithm, called filter back projection, it is possible to reconstruct a virtual slice through the object. When different consecutive slices are reconstructed a 3D visualization can be obtained. This 3D view inside the body or specimen is extremely useful for diagnosing or for research.

The basic idea behind CT is that the internal structure of an object can be reconstructed from multiple projections of the object without destroying it.

The primary elements of X-ray tomography are:

*   An X-ray source

*   A series of detectors that measure X-ray intensity attenuation along multiple beam paths,and

*   A rotational geometry with respect to the object being imaged

Different configurations of these components can be used to create CT scanners optimized for imaging objects of various sizes and compositions.

The great majority of CT systems use X-ray tubes, although tomography can also be done using a synchrotron or gamma-ray emitter as a monochromatic X-ray source. Important tube characteristics are the target material and peak X-ray energy, which determine the X-ray spectrum that is generated; current, which determines X-ray intensity; and the focal spot size, which impacts spatial resolution.

Most CT X-ray detectors utilize scintillators. The parameters that are usually varied are the scintillator material, size and geometry, and the means by which scintillation events are detected and counted. In general, smaller detectors provide better image resolution, but reduced count rates because of their reduced area compared to larger ones. To compensate, longer acquisition times are used to reduce noise levels. Common scintillation materials are cesium iodide, gadolinium oxysulfide, and sodium metatungstate.

1.2.1   Industrial Computed Tomography

The primary difference between Industrial CT and Medical CT is that in Medical CT the object of interest is generally between 1.5 m and 2 m and the composition is of circa 68% water with less heavy elements. However, in the industrial CT the variation of compounds is large because it is used for scanning of industrial components. The scans can vary from millimeters to meters. Additionally, the material can be homogeneous or non-homogeneous materials. All this factors make the Industrial CT-scanner more challenging however, the technology is improving very rapidly.

1.2.2   Micro-CT

Micro computed tomography (micro-CT) is primarily the same as standard CT except it uses a micro focus tube instead of a traditional tube and generally high X-ray energy and also longer exposure time. A micro-CT scan yields resolutions in microns because the focal spot of a micro focus tube is only a few microns in size. For comparison, micro-CT resolution is about 100 times better than the best CAT scan in the medical field.

1.2.3   Image J

ImageJ (Image Processing and Analysis in Java) is a public domain image processing program inspired by the NIH (National Institutes for Health). It can display, analyze, edit and process 8, 16, and 32-bit images and can read file formats such as TIFF and DICOM. It supports a series of images that share a single window; it can calculate distances and perform geometric transformations such as scaling, rotation and flips. Finally, it can be used as a tool to crop and measure images (Image J).

1.3   Noise/Artefacts

The foundations of imaging system performance and image quality can be traced back to the pioneering work of Albert Rose (U.S. National Library of Medicine). He showed that image quality is fundamentally limited by the statistical fluctuations in image quanta. Hence, the more image quanta used to create an image, the better the image quality.

The technology to produce images has improved dramatically during the last decades, but still researchers struggle with artefacts and noise in the image quality. Broadly speaking artefacts is an inherent property i.e. dependent on the X-ray system, whereas noise is an external influence – property that is affected by outside the X-ray system.

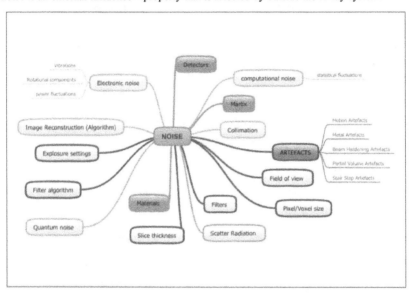

Figure 4: Classification of noise

In the Figure 4 you can see in different colours, the classification of noise. To understand better what effect the different classifications could have on the quality of the data a closer look into each of the elements classified is essential.

1.3.1   Artefacts

An artefact is any error in the perception or representation of any information introduced by the involved equipment or techniques. Only the types of artefacts, which are relevant to this project assignment, are mentioned in detail.

1.3.1.1   Motion Artefacts

These artefacts are introduced by movement of the specimen. Even the slightest of movements of the specimen could produce motion artefacts. In experiments, sometimes this can be a difficult challenge as it may not possible to place a specimen so that it is very stable thus producing artefacts.

To contain this artefact a shorter scanning time should be chosen. Short scanning time could be achieved by for example using a shorter exposure time.

1.3.1.2   Ring Artefacts

This artefact appears due to mis-calibration of one or more detector elements in the CT-Scanner. In this case a new calibration often helps.

1.3.1.3   Metal Artefacts

The presence of metal objects in the scan field can lead to severe artefacts known as streaking. Thisoccurs because the density of the metal is beyond the normal range that can be handled by the current computers, resulting in incomplete profiles. Streaking could be greatly reduced by use of special corrections software.

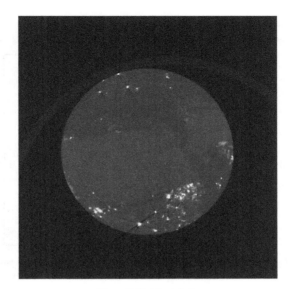

Figure 5: Metal artefacts

1.3.1.4   Beam Hardening Artefacts

Beam hardening is a selective removal of soft X-rays from the X-ray beam. Usually a Gaussian filter is used for removing beam hardening. After removing of soft X-rays the beam becomes more penetrated. The amount of beam hardening required depends on the initial X-ray spectrum as well as on the composition of the material, which is penetrated. If no correction is made, beam hardening artefacts appear as cupping, or a reduction of the reconstructed attenuation coefficient toward the centre of the specimen (University of Texas).

1.3.1.5   Partial Volume Artefacts

There are a number of ways in which the partial volume effect can lead to image artifacts. One type of partial volume artifact occurs when a dense object lying off-center protrudes partway into the width of the x-ray beam. The divergence of the x-ray beam as shown in Figure 6 along the z axis has been greatly exaggerated to demonstrate how such an off-axis object can be within the beam, and therefore "seen" by the detectors, when the tube is pointing from left to right but outside the beam, and therefore not seen by the detectors, when the tube is pointing from right to left. The inconsistencies between the views cause shading artifacts to appear in the image Figure 7.

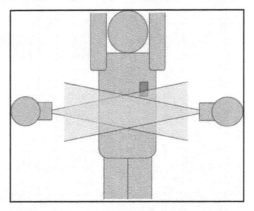

Figure 6: Mechanism of partial volume artifacts, which occur when a dense object lying off-center protrudes part of the way into the x-ray beam(Keat).

Essentially two materials are present in a voxel. Consequently the grey value is an average based on the proportions of the material.

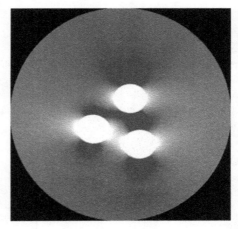

Figure 7: CT images of three 12-mm-diameter acrylic rods supported in air parallel to and approximately 15 cm from the scanner axis. Image obtained with the rods partially intruded into the section width shows partial volume artifacts.

1.3.1.6   Other artefacts

A variety of other artefacts can arise in some situations: stair-step artefact, zebra artefact, helical artefact etc. These are not covered in detail as they are not relevant to this project.

1.3.2   Noise

Real world signals usually contain departures from the ideal signal. Such departures are referred to as noise.

Noise arises as a result of unmodelled or unmodellable processes going on in the production and capture of the real signal.

Noise can generally be grouped into two classes:

*   independent noise

*   noise which is dependent on the image data

One kind of noise which occurs in all recorded images to a certain extent is detector noise. This kind of noise is due to the discrete nature of radiation, i.e. the fact that each imaging system is recording an image by counting photons. A common form of noise is data drop-out noise (commonly referred to as intensity spikes, speckle or salt and pepper noise). Here, the noise is caused by errors in the data transmission.

The corrupted pixels are either set to the maximum value (which looks like snow in the image) or have single bits flipped over. In some cases, single pixels are set alternatively to zero or to the maximum value, giving the image a 'salt and pepper' like appearance. The noise is usually quantified by the percentage of pixels which are corrupted.

1.4   Filters

Filters in general are there to block something, improving image quality by reducing image noise. There are two types of filters: analogue and digital filters.

For this project only digital filters were studied and will be discussed in detail below.

1.4.1   Reasons for using a digital filter

There are three main reasons for using digital filters: Firstly, to separate signals that have been combined. Secondly, to restore signals those have been distorted in same way. Thirdly, to block a frequency or reduce the amplitude of a frequency.

Digital filters are mainly used to suppress:

*   high frequencies in the image (i.e. smoothing the image)

*   low frequencies (i.e. enhancing or detecting edges in the image)

An image can be filtered either in the frequency or in the spatial domain.

1.4.2   High-pass Filters

A high-pass filter, or HPF, passes high frequencies well but attenuates (i.e., reduces the amplitude of) frequencies lower than the filter's cutoff frequency. The actual amount of attenuation for each frequency is a design parameter of the filter. It is also sometimes referred to as a low-cut filter or bass-cut filter (Smith).

1.4.3   Low-pass Filters

This is the most common filter in noise reduction. In contrast to the high-pass filter a low-pass filter passes low-frequency signals but attenuates high-frequency signals. The amount of attenuation depends on the specific low pass filter with specific objectives for example smoothing and blurring of images (Smith).

This work will focus on some of the commonly used low pass filters: the Gaussian Blur filter, Kuwahara filter and Kalman Stack filter.

1.4.4   Kalman Stack Filter

Kalman filter is an optimal estimator or an optimal recursive data processing algorithm. It incorporates all information that can be provided to it. It processes all available measurements, regardless of their precision, to estimate the current value of the variables of interest, with use of knowledge of the system and measurement devices dynamics, the statistical description of the system noise, and uncertainty in the dynamics models, and any available information about initial conditions of the variables of interest. Recursive filter means that Kalman filter does not require all previous date to be kept in storage and reprocessed every time a new measurement is taken. Kalman filter is used for problems, which can be described through a linear model and where noise is white and Gaussian (Maybeck).

1.4.5 Gaussian blur Filter

A Gaussian blur also known as Gaussian smoothing is a low-pass filter. This filter is the result of blurring an image by a Gaussian function. Hence, it is a smoothing filter that alters the characteristics of the image. Mathematically, applying a Gaussian blur to an image is the same as convolving the image with a Gaussian function.

1.4.6 Kuwahara Filter

The Kuwahara filter is an edge-preserving filter that softens the current image but attempts to preserve edges. Similar to the mean filter the Kuwahara filter replaces the current pixel with the mean of a neighbouring 3x3 block that has the least variance. In the Kuwahara Filter, which was used in the experiments the neighbouring could be chosen manually (Kuwahara) .

2 Project Assignment: Analysing noise pattern in Micro-CT

The following section describes the objectives of the project assignment, the results from the experiments, followed by analysis and discussion of the results.

There are many NHM CT projects, which could use noise reduction to improve quantitative analysis of biological/mineralogical structure and composition, which is currently frequently hampered by noise.

This project specifically looked at determining:

I.   How CT-scan parameters can be optimised to reduce noise, and

II.   Which of the many commonly used noise reduction algorithms produce the best results, and

III.   How current and exposure effect each other

The study involved scanning a phantom, formed of glass beads. The phantom was then subsequently imaged using Micro-CT technology to obtain images that provided the raw data for the study of the noise pattern. With the use of imaging software namely CTPro, projections of the phantom were re-constructed. These were then imported into ImageJ software, where the raw data was analysed. A java based plug-in was written for this software as part of the project, which is included in the Appendix.

2.1 Materials and Methods

2.1.1 Metris X-Tek HMX ST 225 CT System

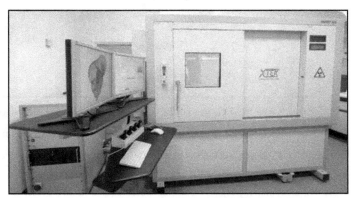

Figure 8: Matrix X-Tek System (NHM)

The system can be used to visualise a wide range of materials:

- **biological** - including chitin, bone and dentine
- **mineralogical** - such as fossils and rock cores
- **man-made** - including plastic, carbon-fibre and metal

Technical details

- Cone beam projection 3 D system
- Four megapixel Perkin Elmer XRD 1621 AN3 HS detector panel
- Volumes constructed using CT PRO (Metris X-Tek, UK) and visualised using VG Studio Max 2.0 (Volume Graphics, Heidelberg, Germany) (NHM research-curation)

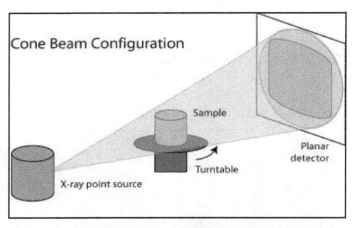

Figure 9: Cone Beam Configuration (Geochemical Instrumentation and Analysis)

The Metris X-Tek HMX ST 225 System is a cone-beam 3 D scanning system.

In cone-beam 3 D scanning, instead of a linear detector a planar detector is used. This allows for the acquisition of the data for an entire object, or a considerable thickness of it, in a single rotation (360°). A cone-beam algorithm is then used to reconstruct the data into images.

The disadvantages of cone-beam 3D scanning are that: the data are subject to some blurring and distortion, the data also shows artefacts stemming from scattering if high-energy X-rays are utilized. However, the advantage of obtaining data for hundreds or thousands of slices at a time is considerable, as more acquisition time can be spent at each turntable position, decreasing image noise Figure 9 (Geochemical Instrumentation and Analysis).

2.1.2   Phantom Design

The Phantom design was composed of glass beads Figure 10 that were covered in flour. These were placed in a plastic flask as shown in Figure 11. The design although, made of simple material – flour – was still challenging, because of its non-homogenous nature. In CT-Scan, because of the non-homogeneity of flour, the noise levels would be higher. For the study, following parameters were chosen: 180 kV, 75 μA, 250 ms were chosen.

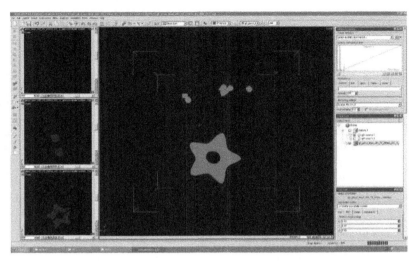

Figure 10: Phantom in VGStudio MAX 2.1

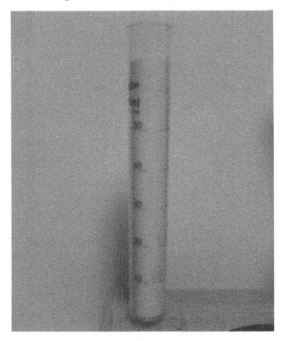

Figure 11: Plastic flask used in the construction of the phantom

Control of x-ray energy and quantity is attained through adjustments of the voltage potential in kilovolts (kV), the x-ray tube current in micro-amperes (µA), and the exposure time in milli-seconds (ms), which are user-adjusted and these depend on the 'target material' (which forms the anode, creating X-rays). The target material could be Silver (Ag), Molybdenum (Mo), Tungsten (W) and Cooper (Cu). The voltage (kV) is very important for good penetration of the specimen. For good penetration the voltage should be high- to accelerate the electrons released by a hot cathode to a high velocity (Seibert). Next, the peak X-ray energy, which determines the X-ray spectrum that is generated, is important. That could be done with current (µA), and exposure (ms). Current determines X-ray intensity, and exposure determines the duration the slice will be penetrated for. The product of exposure duration and current is an important variable (µA- ms). This is referred to as exposure time. The effect of exposure time on noise level will be discussed later in the section.

For the reconstruction process beam hardening 1' and 'noise reduction 1' were chosen. It is not possible in CTPro to reconstruct without any beam hardening or noise reduction. Noise reduction 1 applies no noise reduction algorithm (Ramsey). Only in some scans, reconstruction with a higher beam hardening and noise reduction levels were applied, with the objective to investigate whether the noise reconstruction algorithm in CTpro is better than application of post-reconstruction digital filters.

2.1.3   ImageJ plug-in Code

It is difficult to quantify the quality of the scan. Every scan contains errors. However, the quantification of these errors is a difficult task. To process the images, a plug-in code was written.

Histogram of the scans can be used to quantify the quality of the scans. Histogram describes the distribution of the grey value. Logarithms of the data can reveal large as well as small numbers, which could not be seen in normal distribution. The 3D plot of the ROI is useful for visualization and helps to visualise the noise pattern.

Analysing the histogram gives information on the image noise, specifically the variables: Mean (µ), Standard deviation (σ), and SNR (signal to noise ratio) are important parameters. By, analysing these variables – calculated as well as visualised results – the quality of the scan can be measured and seen. Hence, this all will be a part of the plug-in. In additional the algorithm has to be fast and ROI could be changed manually, so after scanning it can be applied on the data to see whether reconstruction or whether re-scan is required.

The plug-in code is provided in Appendix A.

2.1.3.1   Development of the plug-in

There are already good histogram plug-ins and 3D surface plot plug-in in current version of ImageJ available. However, the parameters required in the project are not calculated. So, the mean, standard deviation, and SNR were added. In addition, flicker, to calculate frame to frame noise, was added as well. The algorithm can be find in the attachment.

2.1.3.2   Using the Plug-in

For a description of how to use the plug-in, refer to section 'How to use the Plug-in'.

2.2   Description of project objectives: Part I, Part II and Part III

2.2.1   Part I: How do scan parameters affect noise?

To study the affect of parameters on the noise, we:

- Designed and fabricated a CT phantom of glass beads in flour as described in detail before. This phantom was then scanned with standard parameters – parameters that were assumed to be reliable and commonly used
- Developed an ImageJ plug-in code to quantify the noise
- Re-scanned the phantom to produce a pattern of noise by varying the parameters:
  - o   X-ray voltage (**kV**) a measure of X-ray penetration
  - o   X-ray current (**μA**) a measure of image brightness / intensity
  - o   X-ray exposure duration (**ms**)

The objective was to validate the pattern of noise variation with the change in the parameters. The affect on noise of each parameter is shown in Figure 12 (arrow indicates general predicted direction of noise increase).

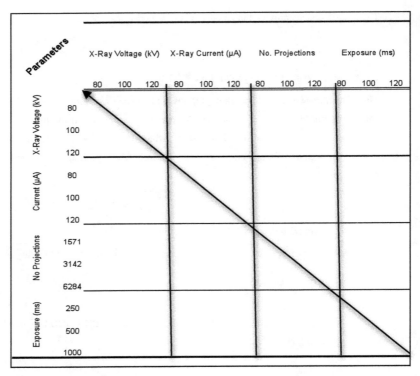

Figure 12: **The above figure shows relationship between voltage, current, exposure duration and noise. The arrow in this figure indicates the noise**

Since the number of possible combinations with the parameters is quite large, this work focussed on investigating few:

- Effect of exposure time (micro-ampere milli-seconds, **µA- ms)** on noise-levels (Jing et. al.) .
- Effect of copper filter (that blocks low density X-rays) on noise levels

Effect of noise reduction algorithm, specifically, for example, comparing whether combination of 'noise reduction level 3' algorithm and a filter (applied post-reconstruction) is better than 'noise reduction level 4' algorithm.

2.2.2   Part II: What is the best type of noise reduction algorithm for CT?

For this section we investigated:

- Selection of the optimum set of scanning parameters (as described before) for the flour and glass phantom
- Testing of noise reduction techniques, for example:
  - Gaussian filter
  - Median filter
  - Kernel filter
  - Fast Fourier Transform (FFT)
  - De-speckling
- Selection of method that produces the best result for noise reduction in relation to partial volume averaging (PVA)

2.2.3   Part III: How current, exposure and noise affect each other?

For this section we investigated:

- Selection of the optimum set of scanning parameters with the same target (Ag) and voltage values but different exposure and current for the flour and glass phantom
- Understand whether the theory widely applied for CT – that describe the relationship between the various scan parameters – holds true for micro-CT as well

CT theory: With higher exposure time (mAs) or higher energy (VAh) the noise level is lower. Increasing tube voltage (kV), tube current (mA) and slice scan time (s) decrease image noise (Hilts).

2.3　　Summary and Analysis

2.3.1　Analysing pattern of the noise variation

The phantom is scanned and the x-ray parameters (X-ray voltage, X-ray current, and X-ray exposure duration) are varied to produce a pattern of noise variation as depicted in Figure 12.

2.3.2　Optmising parameters for noise reduction

The results from the scans are shown in Table 1 shown below. The optimal parameters – that produce the lowest noise without applying any beam hardening or noise reduction in CTPro – were found to be 180 kV, 75 µA, 250 ms exposure duration and with the silver (Ag) as target, and is highlighted below.

Name	kV	uA	expos ure	Target	filter	F to F Noise	Mean	Std. deviation	SNR	Beam Hard	Noise reduct
110_90_250ms_MO_new	110	90	250	MO	No	102.37	4321.84	536.09	8.06	1	1
110_90_250ms_MO_BH2_NR2	110	90	250	MO	No	83.84	2617.71	390.59	6.7	2	2
110_90_250ms_MO_BH2_NR3	110	90	250	MO	No	88.65	2514.2	333.45	7.54	2	3
110_90_250ms_MO_Cu0.1	110	90	250	MO	CU 0.1	77.4	4253.39	605.78	7.02	1	1
180_75_250ms_CU	180	75	250	CU	No	99.5	3675.19	543.78	6.76	1	1
180_75_250ms_W	180	75	250	W	No	100.92	3043.61	521.05	5.84	1	1
180_75_250ms_MO	180	75	250	MO	No	135.2	4556.48	577.31	7.89	1	1
180_75_250ms_AG	180	75	250	AG	No	97.27	5385.72	418.9	12.86	1	1
180_75_250ms_AG_BH4_NR2	180	75	250	AG	No	50.11	2678.41	263.97	10.15	4	2
180_75_250ms_AG_BH4_NR3	180	75	250	AG	No	55.52	2518.59	256.02	9.84	4	3
180_75_250ms_AG_BH4_NR4	180	75	250	AG	No	64.99	2397.5	234.87	10.22	4	4
195_170_250ms_MO_new	195	170	250	MO	No	135.48	4150.33	524.92	7.91	1	1
195_170_250ms_MO_new1	195	170	250	MO	No	145.858	4181.82	513.58	8.14	1	1
195_90_500ms_MO	195	90	500	MO	No	140.32	3865.5	549.99	7.03	1	1
195_60_1000ms_MO	195	60	1000	MO	No	131.85	3414.58	480.78	7.1	1	1
195_60_1000ms_MO_Cu2.5	195	60	1000	MO	CU 2.5	178.89	4512.23	605.54	7.45	1	1

Table 1: Pattern of noise variation

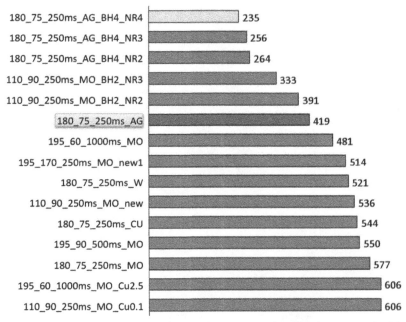

Figure 13: Optimising micro-CT. Highlighted in yellow shows the result with lowest value of standard deviation. Highlighted in orange shows the result with lowest value without beam hardening and noise reduction

This combination will be used to test the filter. For distinction between digital filters with other types of filters – d-filter – is used to underline that it is a digital filter.

2.3.2.1   Effect of noise reduction filters

The following section describes the effect of noise reduction filters.

The noise reduction filters were downloaded from ImageJ homepage (Image J). Due to time constraint, only 20 slices were used. The results are shown in Table below.

Name of filter	F to F Noise	Mean	Standard deviation	SNR	
None	5.58	5427.27	612	8.68	
Accurate Gaussian Blur	5.5	5427.41	256.32	21.17	
Anisotropic Diffusion 2D (sigma 2)	5.57	5425.05	510.57	10.63	ImageJ Page
Hybrid 3D Median Filter	5.62	5422.67	472.28	11.48	
Kalman Stack Filter	4	5423.48	409.44	13.44	
Kuwahara Filter	6.12	5415.73	451.74	11.99	
Mean Shift	5.58	5427.35	613.73	8.84	
Sigma Filter Plus	5.61	5423.79	456.39	11.88	
Gausian Blur	5.5	5427.41	256.32	21.17	
Median	5.9	5414.7	392.24	13.8	
Mean	5.53	5427.34	379.74	14.29	ImageJ Standard
Minimum	10.03	4666.41	386.84	12.06	
Maximum	2.68	6232.42	398.92	15.62	
Unsharp Mask	5.6	5427.2	933.76	5.81	

Table 2: Effect of filter

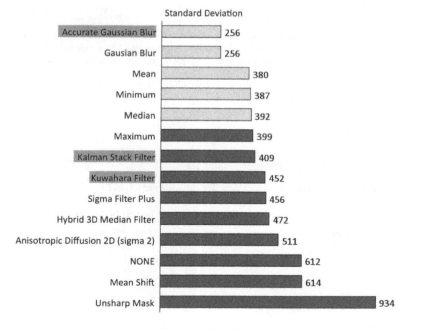

Figure 14: Effect of filters

The results highlighted in yellow are the best five – the one with low noise levels in the comparative sample. However, it was noticed that some of the d-filters made the slices blurry. This is due to the fact that the true value gets replaced with the average or mean of the neighbour's pixel or voxels.

In addition to the noise levels, the resolution and blurriness are important as well. Taking into consideration, both the noise levels and the blurriness of the data, the three filters highlighted in green above give the best results i.e. the Accurate Gaussian Blur, Kalman Stack Filter and Kuwahara Filter.

From all the filtered data a screen shot was taken. This can be found in the appendix.

2.3.2.2   Comparing the filters

In the next step of experiments these three d-filters (Accurate Gaussian Blur, Kalman Stack Filter and Kuwahara Filter) were compared by changing the input parameters. The results are shown below in Table 3.

Name of filter	F to F Noise	Mean	Std. deviation	SNR
180_75_250ms_AG_B&C_AccurateGaussianBlur_1_	96.19	5391.74	310.62	17.36
180_75_250ms_AG_B&C_AccurateGaussianBlur_1.5	96.19	5391.74	245.58	21.96
180_75_250ms_AG_B&C_AccurateGaussianBlur_2	96.2	5391.75	207.32	26
180_75_250ms_AG_B&C_AccurateGaussianBlur_2.5	96.2	5391.76	183.77	29.34
180_75_250ms_AG_B&C_AccurateGaussianBlur_3	96.2	5391.77	168.49	32
180_75_250ms_AG_B&C_Kalman_0.5+0.8	100.35	5389.4	267.49	20.15
180_75_250ms_AG_B&C_Kalman_0.5+0.95192394	108.33	5384.31	190.74	28.23
180_75_250ms_AG_B&C_Kalman_0.048+0.52	97.44	5390.71	366.89	14.69
180_75_250ms_AG_B&C_Kalman_0.048+0.70	98.79	5390.13	307.13	17.55
180_75_250ms_AG_B&C_Kalman_0.048+0.75	99.45	5389.83	287.98	18.71
180_75_250ms_AG_B&C_Kalman_0.048+0.95	108.61	5384.08	189.42	28.42
180_75_250ms_AG_B&C_Kuwahara_1	95.91	5389.75	465.65	11.57
180_75_250ms_AG_B&C_Kuwahara_3	95.91	5389.75	465.65	11.57
180_75_250ms_AG_B&C_Kuwahara_5	95.09	5381.29	385.13	13.97
180_75_250ms_AG_B&C_Kuwahara_7	93.89	5365.84	309.14	17.35
180_75_250ms_AG_B&C_Kuwahara_9	93.07	5354.32	255.31	20.97
180_75_250ms_AG_B&C	96.19	5391.73	480.76	11.22

Table 3: Comparison of the three filters with variation in parameters

The first column is the name of the d-filter with the input parameters. For example, 180_75_250ms_AG_B&C_AccurateGaussianBlur_1.5 refers to 180kV, 75µA, 250ms, silver (Ag) target with Accurate Gaussian filter (with average value of 1.5).

2.3.2.3   Optimum noise reduction algorithm

To determine which of three above-mentioned filters is the best, resolution and blurriness were eliminated. The results can be seen in the Table 4 below. The best three results are highlighted.

Name of filter	F to F Noise	Mean	Std. deviation	SNR
180_75_250ms_AG_B&C_AccurateGaussianBlur_1	96.19	5391.74	310.62	17.36
180_75_250ms_AG_B&C_Kalman_0.5+0.8	100.35	5389.4	267.49	20.15
180_75_250ms_AG_B&C_Kalman_0.048+0.52	97.44	5390.71	366.89	14.69
180_75_250ms_AG_B&C_Kalman_0.048+0.70	98.79	5390.13	307.13	17.55
180_75_250ms_AG_B&C_Kalman_0.048+0.75	99.45	5389.83	287.98	18.71
180_75_250ms_AG_B&C_Kuwahara_1	95.91	5389.75	465.65	11.57
180_75_250ms_AG_B&C_Kuwahara_3	95.91	5389.75	465.65	11.57
180_75_250ms_AG_B&C_Kuwahara_5	95.09	5381.29	385.13	13.97

Table 4: Results of noise reduction filters. The best results are highlighted

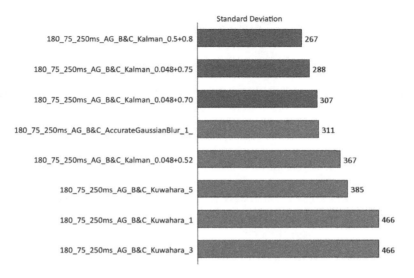

Figure 15: Kalman Stack filter gives best results (low standard deviation)

- Accurate Gaussian Blur: With input Sigma (Radius) higher than 1 the scans are blurry. Only the one with Sigma 1 gives the best result
- Kalman Stack Filter: Only one of the dataset is a bit blurry. This is eliminated.
- Kawahara Filter: With Sampling window width higher than 5 the edges are jagged. Hence, the limitation will be made to 5.

The analysis indicated that Kalman d-filter works the best for noise reduction. Based on these results the Kalman Stack Filter is suggested.

2.3.2.4   Comparison between Kalman stack filter with the reduction algorithm in CTpro

A comparison between the Kalman Stack Filter and noise reduction algorithm in CTpro were made. The objective was to investigate whether the in-built noise reduction algorithm in CTpro is better compared with the Kalman Stack Filter. The Table 5 shows the results of the experiment.

Name of filter	F to F Noise	Mean	Std. deviation	SNR
180_75_250ms_AG_BH4_NR3	54.81	2532.82	280.35	9.03
180_75_250ms_AG_BH4_NR2_Kalman_0.03+0.75	51.37	2681.38	179.1	14.97
180_75_250ms_AG_BH4_NR4	64.99	2397.5	234.57	10.22
180_75_250ms_AG_BH4_NR3_Kalman_0.028+0.75	56.42	2531.51	170.38	14.86
110_90_250ms_MO_BH2_NR3	85.66	2519.29	336.26	7.47
110_90_250ms_MO_BH2_NR2_Kalman_0.037+0.75	82.87	2621.97	214.58	12.13

Table 5: Comparison between CTpro noise reduction algorithm and Kalman filter

The results indicate that the Kalman Stack Filter has lower noise levels compared with the in-built noise reduction algorithm in CTPro.

2.3.3   Analysing current vs. exposure effect

Current (in µA) and exposure (in ms) are user defined while carrying out the experiments. Hence, it is of fundamental importance to understand the impact of these on the scans. However in literature, there are two theories describing the effect of current and exposure on the image quality, that contradict each other.

In the first theory, it has been documented that lower the value of current (mA) or the exposure duration (ms), higher will be noise (Jing et. al.) (i.e. current or exposure and noise are directly proportional).Whereas the second source states that the noise (as described by standard deviation), is inversely proportional to the root of them, A-S, (Kramme). The two results are in direct conflict with each other. Further, literature review did not yield any results to support or disprove one theory over the other. To clarify the effect of current and exposure on the noise (i.e. standard deviation), experiments and the subsequent theoretical analysis were carried out.

Figure 16 shows, the results of 9 scans, the corresponding current and exposure with the level of noise or standard deviation. In two scans the current is kept constant (at 60µA) whilst the exposure is varied (354 seconds and 500 seconds). The results show a negative correlation – with increasing exposure in milli-seconds the standard deviation decreases (from 459 to 437). These results are similar to that supported by the first theory (Jing et. al.) .

A similar set of experiments were carried out to understand the effect of current on the image quality whilst keeping the exposure (in milli-seconds) constant. Experiments were carried out with a constant exposure value of 250 milli-seconds. The current values for these three scans were kept at 75, 90 and 130µAs. These results support the second theory (Kramme), increasing the current increases the standard deviation, (419, 426 and 458 respectively).

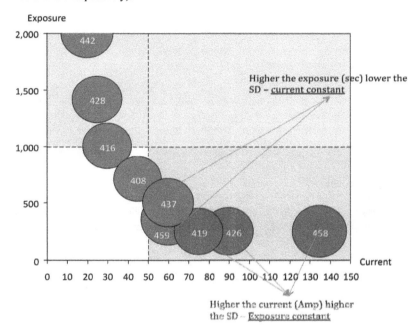

Figure 16: Effect of current and exposure on noise. The number inside the bubbles indicate the standard deviation value.

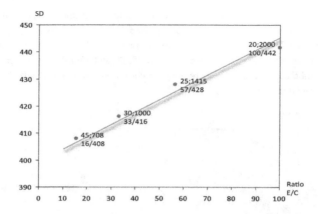

Figure 17: SD vs Ratio of Exposure to current (ms/µA) between 708 and 2000 ms exposure. The top numbers in each represent the current value and exposure time. The bottom number shows the ratio / standard deviation

Figure 17 plots the standard deviation and the corresponding ratio of exposure to current (ms/µA). If we look at the exposure from 708 ms to 2000 ms a trend is visible. As the ratio increases the standard deviation becomes larger i.e. the data becomes noisier.

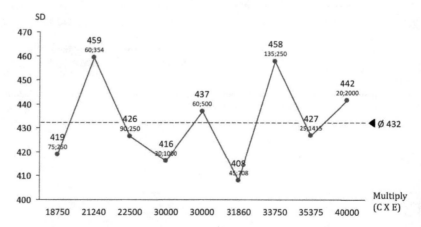

Figure 18: SD vs exposure time, no trend between exposure time and standard deviation

Figure 18 plots, the standard deviation and the corresponding product of exposure and current The data shows that there is no trend between noise (standard deviation) and exposure time (in μA-ms).

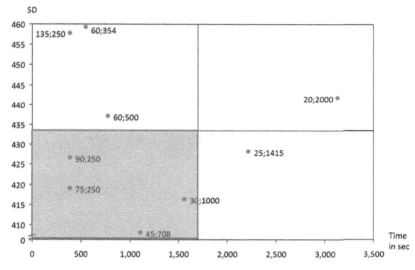

Figure 19: time = scanning time plotted against SD

Figure 19 shows the results of scanning time and the corresponding standard deviation. The data suggests that for exposure time less than 1000 ms the scans have a much lower value of standard deviation or lower value of noise.

Theory suggests that increasing kV is a more efficient means of improving image noise than increasing mA or s since load on the x-ray tube is given by: kJ = kV * mA *s. As such, maximizing kV should be top priority for scan technique.(Hilts). To test whether high Voltage (kV) and/or height energy (kJ) lover noise, scans were carried out as shown in Figure 20, with Molybdenum (Mo) as the target. The theory could not be proven by the test.

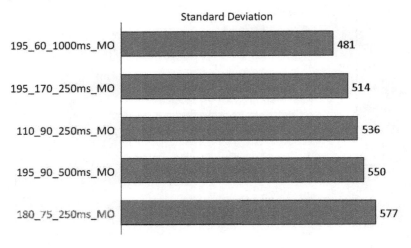

Standard Deviation

195_60_1000ms_MO	481
195_170_250ms_MO	514
110_90_250ms_MO	536
195_90_500ms_MO	550
180_75_250ms_MO	577

Figure 20: Set of scans with Mo target and different Voltage, current and exposure. First number is voltage (kV) second is current (µA), next is exposure (ms) and target (Mo)

3   Conclusion and future work

The following section briefly summarises the overall conclusions of this thesis. In addition, some recommendations are made for future work.

3.1   Insight from experiments

The experiments give the following insights:

*   While using silver (Ag) target it was found that optimum values of parameters are 180Kv, 75 µA, 250 ms exposure duration.

*   Furthermore, it was found that a higher value of the current leads to noisier scans. The critical point of current was found to be 60 µA. Any change – low exposure and higher current or higher exposure and lower current – the standard deviation starts to grow or the scans become noisier.

It was found that silver (Ag) is a better target for $CaIO_3$, and could be preferable for bones and shell as well.

My suggestions for scanning parameters for similar specimens:

*   First, voltage should be kept high at 180 kV

*   It is suggested to use silver (Ag) as the target

*   If possible current should be set at 50 µA and only exposure is varied. If it is not possible to achieve this varied of current the current could be set at 75 µA.

3.2   Insights from post-processing

The image analysis also gave some valuable insight:

*   The digitial filter – Kalman Stack Filter – gave the best results for the scan

*   Kalman Stack Filter was also found to give better results compared with propriety filter that is provided with CTPro software

3.3 Suggestions for future work:

1. As discussed in 2.3.3, the behaviour at a critical current of 60 μA needs to be investigated further. To achieve these further experiments could be designed.

   a. Using other targets: The experiments presented in this work were done only with silver target. It may be useful to see if the experiment is repeatable with other targets as well. It is also likely that each target may have a different critical current. It could then be concluded from the results whether, the phenomenon – at low exposure and higher current or higher exposure and lower current the standard deviation starts to grow or the scans become noisier – is independent of the target an hence is an internal property of the micro-CT system, or is dependent on the target.

2. As discussed in section 2.3.3 it is important to further understand the departure of the results from theory. It may be useful to design experiments with same target and understanding which of the parameters, (kV, μA, ms) has the biggest influence on the image quality. These experiments could be:

   a. The current in the experiment could be kept same, whilst the variations in voltage and exposure are studied

   b. The voltage and current in the experiment could be kept same, whilst the exposure is studied

   c. The exposure in the experiment could be kept same, whilst the variations in voltage and current are studied

   d. The voltage and exposure in the experiment could be kept same, whilst the current is studied

Developing relationship charts of voltage, current and exposure can aid in understanding the departure from the theory. This will help to illustrate amongst other things, whether the theory for CT applies directly to micro-CT as well or the behaviour at micro level is inconsistent with CT level.

Appendix A

Plug-in Code

```java
import java.awt.*;
import java.awt.Panel;
import java.awt.Button;
import java.awt.event.*;
import javax.swing.*;
import ij.*;
import ij.gui.*;
import ij.plugin.filter.*;
import ij.process.*;
import ij.gui.WaitForUserDialog;

/**
 *      This ImageJ plugin calculates the 1D and 3D-noise from a
ROI.
 *
 *      Useage:
 *      1) Open an image sequence and selects an ROI.
 *      2) Run this plug-in
 *      3) Verify the ROI.
 *
 *   This plugin was developed to analyze the 3D-noise or 1D-
noise
 *      in Micro-CT scannes.
 *
 *      Output:
 *      The ImageJ Results Window is loaded with
 *      a) Mean
 *      b) Standard deviation
 *      c) SNR
 *      d) Size of the "Data Cube": height, width, # frames
 *
 *      Author = Galina Bernahrdt, NHM London 2010
 */

public class Noise_quantity implements PlugInFilter,
ActionListener {

int iX;
int iY;
```

```
intiXROI;
intiYROI;
intiSlice;
int            Nt;
intNv;
intNh;
booleanbAbort;
ImagePlusimp;
char Tab;
char        Sigma;
GenericDialogTheGD;
Rectangle      r;
ButtonTheButton;

/**
 *      Called by ImageJ when the filter is loaded
 */
publicint setup(String arg, ImagePlus imp) {
this.imp = imp;
if (arg.equals("about"))
               {showAbout(); returnDONE;}
if (IJ.versionLessThan("1.39r")) returnDONE;
returnDOES_8G+DOES_16+DOES_32+ROI_REQUIRED+NO_CHANGES;
    }

/**
 *      Called by ImageJ to process the image
 */
publicvoid run(ImageProcessor ip) {
bAbort = false;
r = ip.getRoi();
Nt = imp.getNSlices();
Nv = r.height;
Nh = r.width;
iXROI = r.x;
iYROI = r.y;
iSlice = imp.getCurrentSlice();
Tab = (char)9;
Sigma = (char)963;


//#################################################
//Ask User to verify the Region of Interest (ROI) to analyze
get3DnoiseROI();
if (bAbort)
return;
iX = iXROI;
```

```
iY = iYROI;
//Display the ROI as a rectangle on the image
imp.setRoi(iX, iY, Nh, Nv);


//#################################################
//Place the ROI into a 3D array Stvh, the "data cube"
int t, v, h, cSlice;
double[][][] Stvh = newdouble[Nt][Nv][Nh];
cSlice = imp.getCurrentSlice();
for(t=0; t<Nt; t++) {
     imp.setSlice(t+1);
     for(v=0; v<Nv; v++) {
     for(h=0; h<Nh; h++) {
          Stvh[t][v][h] = (double)ip.getPixel(iX+h,iY+v);
            }
     }
      }
imp.setSlice(cSlice);

//#################################################
//Calculate 3D Noise using the "data cube"
double[] farray = newdouble[Nt];
for(v=0; v<Nv; v++) {
     for(h=0; h<Nh; h++) {

     for(t=0; t<Nt; t++) {

     farray[t] = Stvh[t][v][h];}


//****************************
// Calculate S
double S = Mean1D( Make1D(Stvh) );
     for(t=0; t<Nt; t++) {
          for(v=0; v<Nv; v++) {
               for(h=0; h<Nh; h++) {
                    Stvh[t][v][h] -= S;
               }//for
          }//for
     }//for


//****************************
//Calculate standard deviation (average)

double StandD = sdKnuth(farray);
```

```
//***************************
//Calculate flicker
double[][][] MUt = newdouble[Nt][1][1];
        MUt = Mean3D( Mean3D( Stvh, 2), 3);
double SIGt = sdKnuth( Make1D(MUt) );
for(t=0; t<Nt; t++) {
     for(v=0; v<Nv; v++) {
     for(h=0; h<Nh; h++) {
          Stvh[t][v][h] -= MUt[t][0][0];
             }
     }
       }


//***************************
// Calculate SNR
double SNR = (S/sdKnuth(farray));



//***************************
//Display the results
IJ.getTextPanel();
IJ.setColumnHeadings("---"+Tab+"image units"+Tab+"Meaning");
//Pot
     IJ.write(""+Tab+IJ.d2s(SIGt,6)+Tab+"Frame to frame noise
or bounce (flicker)");
IJ.write(""+Tab+IJ.d2s(S,3)+Tab+"Average Gray Value (Mean)");
IJ.write(""+Tab+IJ.d2s(StandD,4)+Tab+"Standard deviation
(average)");
IJ.write(""+Tab+IJ.d2s(SNR,4)+Tab+"SNR");
IJ.write(""+Tab+Nt+Tab+"Frames");
IJ.write(""+Tab+Nv+Tab+"Rows");
IJ.write(""+Tab+Nh+Tab+"Columns");

IJ.register(Noise_quantity_.class);
     }

/**
     *     Creates a dialog box, allowing the user to enter the
requested
     *     width, height, x & y coordinates for a Region Of
Interest.
     *          (From the ImageJ plugin "Specify_ROI" by Anthony
Padua)
```

```
    */
void get3DnoiseROI() {

GenericDialog gd = newGenericDialog("Analysis ROI",
IJ.getInstance());
gd.addNumericField("Width:", Nh, 0);
gd.addNumericField("Height:", Nv, 0);
gd.addNumericField("X Coordinate:", iXROI, 0);
gd.addNumericField("Y Coordinate:", iYROI, 0);

gd.showDialog();

if (gd.wasCanceled()) {
bAbort = true;
return;
        }

Nh = (int) gd.getNextNumber();
Nv = (int) gd.getNextNumber();
iXROI = (int) gd.getNextNumber();
iYROI = (int) gd.getNextNumber();
    }


publicvoid actionPerformed(ActionEvent e)

// Detect and handle user interactions with buttons and other
window objects.
{
    if (e.getSource()==TheButton)
    {

        TheGD.dispose();
    }
}


/**
 * Calculates the standard deviation of an array of numbers.
 * see Knuth's The Art Of Computer Programming
 * Volume II: Seminumerical Algorithms
 * This algorithm is slower, but more resistant to error
propagation.
 *
 * @param data Numbers to compute the standard deviation of.
 * Array must contain two or more numbers.
 * @return standard deviation estimate of population
```

```
    * ( to get estimate of sample, use n instead of n-1 in last
line )
    */
double sdKnuth ( double[] data )
      {
finalint n = data.length;
if ( n < 2 )
          {
returnDouble.NaN;
          }
double avg = data[0];
double sum = 0;
for ( int i = 1; i < data.length; i++ )
          {
double newavg = avg + ( data[i] - avg ) / ( i + 1 );
sum += ( data[i] - avg ) * ( data [i] -newavg ) ;
avg = newavg;
          }
returnMath.sqrt( sum / ( n - 1 ) );
      }


/**
    * Calculates the mean of an 1D array
    */
double Mean1D ( double[] data )
      {
int n = data.length;
if ( n < 1 )
          {
returnDouble.NaN;
          }
double avg = data[0];
double sum = 0;
for ( int i = 1; i < data.length; i++ )
          {
sum += data[i];
          }
return ( sum/n );
      }

/**
    * Calculates the mean of a 3D array and
    * returns the result as a 3D array where the dimension
    * being averaged has been reduced to unity.
    */
double[][][] Mean3D ( double[][][] data, int dim )
```

```
      {
int i1=0, i2=0, i3=0;
int d1=0, d2=0, d3=0;
int N1 = data.length;
int N2 = data[0].length;
int N3 = data[0][0].length;
double sum=0;

if( dim==1 ) {
     d1=1; d2=N2; d3=N3;
        }
if( dim==2 ) {
     d1=N1; d2=1; d3=N3;
        }
if( dim==3 ) {
     d1=N1; d2=N2; d3=1;
        }
double[][][] TheAve = newdouble[d1][d2][d3];

if( dim==1 ) {
     for(i2=0; i2<N2; i2++) {
     for(i3=0; i3<N3; i3++) {
          sum=0;
          for(i1=0; i1<N1; i1++) {
          sum += data[i1][i2][i3];
          }
          TheAve[0][i2][i3] = sum/N1;
            }
     }
        }
if( dim==2 ) {
     for(i1=0; i1<N1; i1++) {
     for(i3=0; i3<N3; i3++) {
          sum=0;
          for(i2=0; i2<N2; i2++) {
          sum += data[i1][i2][i3];
          }
          TheAve[i1][0][i3] = sum/N2;
            }
     }
        }
if( dim==3 ) {
     for(i1=0; i1<N1; i1++) {
     for(i2=0; i2<N2; i2++) {
          sum=0;
          for(i3=0; i3<N3; i3++) {
          sum += data[i1][i2][i3];
```

```
                    }
                    TheAve[i1][i2][0] = sum/N3;
                        }
            }
                }

    return ( TheAve );
        }


/**
    * Inputs a 3D array and outputs a 1D array.
    */
double[] Make1D ( double[][][] data )
        {
int n=0;
int i1=0, i2=0, i3=0;
int N1 = data.length;
int N2 = data[0].length;
int N3 = data[0][0].length;

double[] The1Darray = newdouble[N1*N2*N3];
for(i1=0;i1<N1;i1++) {
        for(i2=0; i2<N2; i2++) {
        for(i3=0; i3<N3; i3++) {
                The1Darray[n] = data[i1][i2][i3];
                n++;
                    }
        }
            }
return ( The1Darray );
        }



/**
        *        Displays a short message describing the filter
        */
void showAbout() {
IJ.showMessage("About Calculate_3Dnoise...",
"This PlugIn performs a 3D-Noise Analysis on a specified ROI.\n"
        );
    }

}
```

How to use the Plug-in

To start and use the ImageJ plug-in a copy of .class file has to be coped to the Plugins folder in ImageJ and a restart of the program is necessary. First, the image sequences are imported. The program is a fast algorithm, and works only on a stack of input slices. Hence, the input of the slices should be higher than 2.

Second, choose a "rectangular" toll and choose a ROI (region of interest) in your slices. The selection of the ROI is done as shown in the image below (yellow region).

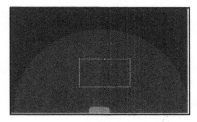

Figure 21: Selecting the region of interest

Then load the plug-in, which contains the plug-in code (noise_quantity) written for analysis as described previously. A small window appears. At this stage if needed the ROI can be modified by manual input through the plug-in as shown inFigure 22. When the required modifications are complete the algorithm is processed by pressing OK.

Figure 22: Manual modification of the parameters can be done if needed

After the completion of the processing a window with results appears as shown in Figure 23.

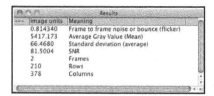

Figure 23: Results from the scan

References

Geochemical Instrumentation and Analysis. http://serc.carleton.edu/research_education/geochemsheets/techniques/CT.html. 25 June 2010.

Hilts, M. and Duzenli, C. "Image noise in X-ray CT polymer gel dosimetry." 2004.

Hubpages London. http://hubpages.com/hub/A-London-visit-on-the-cheap-5-free-family-activities. 2010. 25 July 2010.

Image J. http://rsbweb.nih.gov/ij/. 05 June 2010.

Jing et. al. "An experimental study on the noise properties of X-ray CT sinogram data in Radon space." 2008.

Karthikeyan, D and Chegy. Deepa. Step by Step CT Scan . Anshan Ltd, 2006.

Keat, Julia F. Barrett and Nicholas. "Artefacts in CT: Recognition and Avoidance." RadioGraphics 2004, vol. 24 no. 6 ed.

Kramme. "Medizintechnik." Kramme. Medizintechnik 3. Auflage. Springer Medizin Verlag Heidelberg, 2007. 266.

Kuwahara. http://rsbweb.nih.gov/ij/plugins/kuwahara.html. 21 June 2010.

Maybeck, Peter S. Stochastic models, estimation, and control. 1st Edition. London: Academic Press, 1979.

NHM. http://www.nhm.ac.uk/research-curation/science-facilities/analytical-imaging/imaging/computed-tomography/micro-ct/instrument/index.html. 13 June 2010.

NHM research-curation. http://www.nhm.ac.uk/research-curation/science-facilities/analytical-imaging/imaging/computed-tomography/micro-ct/instrument/index.html. 13 June 2010.

Ramsey, Andrew. pers. comm. with X-Trek engineer

Seibert, J.A. "X-Ray Imaging Physics for Nuclear Medicine Technologists. Part 1: Basic Principles of X-Ray Productions." Journal of Nuclear Medicine Technology 32.3 (2004): 139-147.

Smith, Steven W. Digital Signal Processing - A practical Guide for Engineers and Scientists. Newnws, 2003.

Thackray, John and Bob Press. Nature's Treasurehouse. London: The Natural History Museum, 2001.

U.S. National Library of Medicine. http://www.ncbi.nlm.nih.gov/pubmed/10069050. 17 July 2010.

University of Texas. http://www.ctlab.geo.utexas.edu/overview/index.php#anchor5-2. 15 July 2010.

Wikipedia Natural History Museum. http://en.wikipedia.org/wiki/Natural_History_Museum. 19 July 2010. 25 July 2010.

www.ingramcontent.com/pod-product-compliance
Lightning Source LLC
LaVergne TN
LVHW042259060326
832902LV00009B/1129